4D

AN AUGMENTED REALITY
SCIENCE EXPERIENCE

CURIOUS PEARL
SCIENCE GIRL

CURIOUS PEARL
OBSERVES MIGRATION

by Eric Braun

illustrated by Stephanie Dehennin

PICTURE WINDOW BOOKS

a capstone imprint

Curious Pearl here! Do you like science? I sure do! I have all sorts of fun tools to help me observe and investigate, but my favorite tool is my science notebook. That's where I write down questions and facts that help me learn more about science. Would you like to join me on my science adventures? You're in for a special surprise!

Download the Capstone 4D app!

Videos for all of the sidebars in this book are at your fingertips with the 4D app.

To download the Capstone 4D app:
- Search in the Apple App Store or Google Play for "Capstone 4D"
- Click Install (Android) or Get, then Install (Apple)
- Open the application
- Scan any page with this icon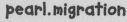

You can also access the additional resources on the web at www.capstone4D.com using the password **pearl.migration**

CURIOUS PEARL

SCIENCE GIRL

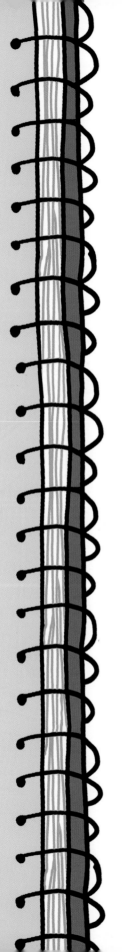

Saturdays are "Sal days." I get to visit my friend Sal.

"Hey, Sal!" I said. "What's wrong?"

"All summer long, pretty yellow birds called warblers nested in my yard," he said. "But now they're gone. I guess I spooked them."

"It's fall," I said. "Maybe they're back in school." I nudged him with my elbow and giggled to myself.

But Sal was not in the mood for jokes.

"Sorry," I said. "I'm sure they didn't leave because of you. Let's see if we can solve this mystery." I pulled out my notebook and pencil.

"We'll never figure it out," replied Sal.

"Come on, Sal. Let's try!" I said.

"OK," said Sal. "I'm in. What do we do?"

"Well, what would a scientist do?" I asked.

"Observe!" answered Sal.

"Eureka!" I said. That's a super scientific word! I use it when I'm excited about discovering something new. "Let's go!"

We headed out to the woods to learn about
animal behavior.

"Check out those squirrels," said Sal.

"They're gathering seeds and acorns," I replied.
"They need food for winter."

"And those beavers are building a lodge in the
stream," said Sal. "They need a safe place to live."

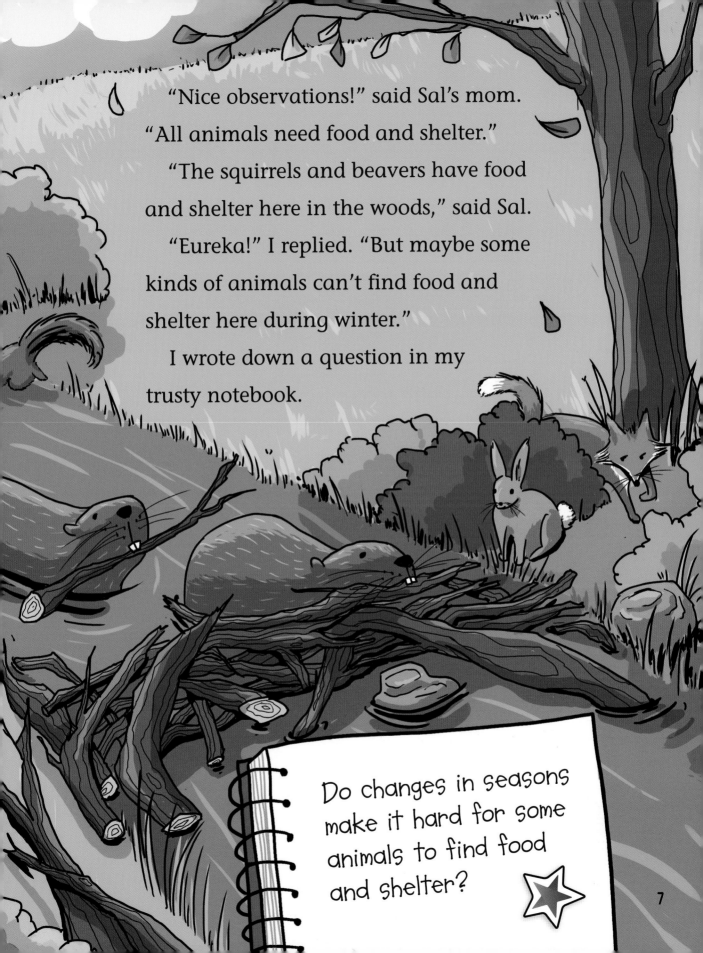

"Nice observations!" said Sal's mom. "All animals need food and shelter."

"The squirrels and beavers have food and shelter here in the woods," said Sal.

"Eureka!" I replied. "But maybe some kinds of animals can't find food and shelter here during winter."

I wrote down a question in my trusty notebook.

Do changes in seasons make it hard for some animals to find food and shelter?

We headed back to Sal's house and sat down on the patio.

"So where do warblers find shelter?" I asked.

"They used to hang around in those bushes," Sal said. "Before they got mad at me and left."

"Don't be silly," I said. "They didn't get mad. Look! The bushes are losing their leaves. Winter is coming!"

"Do you see those goldfinches?" I asked. "Did the warblers like your bird feeder too?"

"No," Sal said. "They eat bugs. They find them in the bushes where they nest."

"Eureka!" I said. "Bugs are like leaves. They are harder to find in winter."

"Just like yellow warblers," Sal said.

I opened my notebook and wrote down another question.

How do animals find shelter and food in winter?

"What else happens in winter?" I asked Sal.

"Indoor soccer season!" he said.

"No!" I said. "I'm talking about the weather."

"Oh, you mean it gets cold," he said. "And the cute little yellow warblers go away."

"Eureka! It gets cold." I replied. "We can put on hats and jackets, but birds can't. My mom once told me that birds fluff up their feathers to stay warm."

"That makes sense, Pearl!" said Sal.

I wrote this down in my notebook.

How do birds stay warm in winter? Some birds fluff up and trap body heat in their feathers.

"It's time to find some answers to our questions," I said.

"I have a question," Sal said. "Do you want to play soccer?"

"Later," I said. "Don't you want to figure out what happened to the warblers?"

"All I know is they're gone," Sal said. "And they're not coming back."

"Follow me," I told him.

Sal and I headed inside. I grabbed our tablet and typed *warblers* into the search engine. It pulled up information for us.

"Look," I said. "It says here that warblers fly south in winter. It's called migration."

I wrote down the definition of *migrate* in my notebook.

When animals migrate, they move to another area to find food and shelter.

"The warblers will come back in spring," I
said. "Then they'll find bugs and live in the leafy
bushes."

"Awesome!" he said.

Sal pointed to the screen. "Look," he said. "The
answer to all of your questions has to do with the
weather. It says here that in Central America it
stays warmer in winter. The leaves don't drop, so
warblers can safely nest in bushes. The bugs eat
the leaves, and warblers eat the bugs."

"Eureka!" I replied. "That's it, Sal!"

"It says here that in spring it gets too hot down south," I said. "The warblers fly north again."

"That sounds like a lot of work," Sal said. "Do all animals do that?"

"I don't know," I said.

"Salmon," said Sal's mom as she offered us a plate.

"Salmon sandwiches?" Sal asked. "Yuck!"

"No," she said. "Salmon migrate. We used to see them in a stream when I was your age. They live in the ocean and swim upstream to lay eggs. The stream has less predators, so it's a safer place to lay eggs."

"That makes sense," I said.

I wrote down a note about salmon.

Some animals, like salmon, migrate to lay eggs or breed.

"It sounds like there are lots of reasons animals migrate," Sal said. "To find food. To find shelter."

"To find a safe place to breed or raise their young," Sal's mom said.

We looked up other migrating animals online. We found out that zebras travel almost 2,000 miles (3,219 kilometers) every year to find fresh grass and water!

We learned that all sorts of animals migrate: butterflies, birds, insects, deer, snakes, sharks, bats, elephants, and frogs. Geese, crabs, and earthworms also migrate. Caribou migrate too. I made a note in my notebook.

Caribou migrate to find food and give birth to their young.

Sal said, "I'm glad the warblers will be back."

"In spring," I said. "Meanwhile, will you show me how to make a bird feeder like yours?"

"Sure," he said.

"Great!" I said. "I'm excited to see whatever kind of birds migrate my way!"

People and Animals Migrate

1. Think of any family members or friends you know who have moved to a different city. Write down their names on a sheet of paper.

2. Ask an adult if you can call or e-mail as many of them as possible. Ask each of them to explain the reasons why they moved.

3. Make a chart that shows people's reasons for moving.

4. Ask an adult to help you research migrating animals online. Make a list of as many migrating animals as possible. Explain why the animals migrate.

5. Do people and animals migrate for the same reasons? What are some connections you see? Tell an adult about your findings.

GLOSSARY

behavior—the way a person or animal acts

breed—to mate and produce young

Central America—a tropical region that connects North America and South America

eureka—a cry of joy or satisfaction

lodge—a beaver's home of mud, logs, and sticks, built in the water

migrate—to move from one place to another

migration—the regular movement of animals from one place to another as they search for food or resources

observation—something you have noticed by watching carefully

observe—to watch something closely in order to learn something

predator—an animal that hunts other animals for food

shelter—a place where an animal can stay safe from weather and other animals

warbler—a small, American songbird; the yellow warbler is one kind

READ MORE

Bader, Bonnie. *Fly, Butterfly.* New York: Grosset & Dunlap, an imprint of Penguin Group (USA) LLC, 2014.

Katz Cooper, Sharon. *When Whales Cross the Sea: The Gray Whale Migration.* North Mankato, Minnesota: Picture Window Books, 2015.

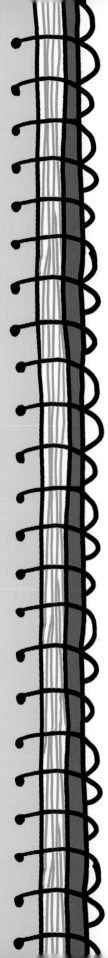

INTERNET SITES

Use FactHound to find Internet sites related to this book.

Visit *www.facthound.com*

Just type in 9781515813446 and go.

CRITICAL THINKING QUESTIONS

What are three reasons that an animal might migrate?

Some animals migrate very long distances. What are some challenges they might face on such a long journey?

Can people migrate? Why or why not? Give an example.

MORE BOOKS IN THE SERIES

INDEX

Thanks to our adviser for his expertise, research, and advice:
Christopher T. Ruhland, PhD
Professor of Biological Sciences
Department of Biology
Minnesota State University, Mankato

Editor: Shelly Lyons
Designer: Ted Williams
Art Director: Nathan Gassman
Production Specialist: Katy LaVigne
The illustrations in this book were digitally produced.

Picture Window Books are published by Capstone, 1710 Roe Crest Drive, North Mankato, Minnesota 56003
www.mycapstone.com

Library of Congress Cataloging-in-Publication Data
Cataloging-in-Publication information is on file with Library of Congress.
Names: Braun, Eric, author. | Dehennin, Stephanie, illustrator.
Title: Curious Pearl Observes Migration: 4D
ISBN 978-1-5158-1344-6 (library binding)
ISBN 978-1-5158-1348-4 (paperback)
ISBN 978-1-5158-1360-6 (eBook PDF)

Printed and bound in the USA.
010373F17